I0408911

Travel, Lead, Earn

Your Step-by-Step Guide to Become a TripLeader

Navigate from passionate explorer to profitable TripLeader, turning your love for travel into income, without compromise.

By

Nico Estinto

TABLE OF CONTENTS

Transforming Passion into Profit

Welcome to "Travel, Lead, Earn: Your Step-by-Step Guide to Become a Trip Leader", your comprehensive roadmap to converting your passion for traveling into a source of income. If your heart races at the thought of traveling the world, meeting interesting people, and creating unforgettable memories, all while earning money, then you've come to the right place!

This e-book is your golden ticket to mastering the art of becoming a TripLeader – the savvy digital nomad who earns while guiding others on breathtaking adventures without leaving their main job. This guide is not just filled with practical tips and step-by-step strategies; it's also peppered with real-life experiences and insights that will inspire and motivate you... And we assure you, it's a ride worth taking!

We'll show you how to plan, promote, and conduct trips that will not just mesmerize your travel buddies, but also leave them looking forward to more. We'll delve deep into the art of mastering digital platforms, negotiating, and budget-setting, while also focusing on the personal growth and leadership skills required to lead successful trips.

This is not just a guide; it's a window into an exhilarating lifestyle that blends work, travel, and fun into a cocktail of unforgettable experiences. We're talking about a life where your passion pays for every single trip, where your office could be a beachside café in Bali or a bustling plaza in the heart of Malaga.

So, buckle up, future TripLeaders, It's time to turn the next page and step into a world where you get paid to travel, make friends, and build a lifetime of memories — all of it without sacrificing your job. Your adventure can begin now!

1.1 Unmatched Appeal of the Digital Nomad Lifestyle

Greetings, adventurous soul! If you've found yourself unable to quench your wanderlust with just a two-week, all-inclusive "**Workation** (work-vacation)", then you're in the right place. Here, we go beyond the ordinary — we take vacations to the next level. We're talking about transforming your wanderlust into a fulfilling and profitable lifestyle by organizing trips and traveling with other like-minded people. So, fasten your seatbelts for the journey of a lifetime.

Over recent years, the digital nomad trend has surged from being a daring ripple in the world of work to a colossal wave. What was once regarded as unconventional or even absurd, is now as mainstream as your favorite cup of Starbucks' Latte.

The work landscape has evolved, breaking away from the traditional office cubicles. Now, armed with a laptop and a decent internet connection, you can work from a quaint café in Paris, a sun-drenched beach in Mallorca, or a cabin overlooking the snow-capped Swiss mountains. Exciting, isn't it?

1.2 Navigating This Guide

Now that we've whetted your appetite for adventure, let's delve into the details of this guide.

Consider this guide as a treasure map — not just a leisure read, but a journey that could transform your life into an exhilarating blend of exploration, connection, and profitability.

Each chapter immerses you deeper into the intriguing world of the digital nomad lifestyle and the rewarding life of a **TripLeader**. This guide will accompany you through the realms of remote work, co-working trips, and leveraging your passion for travel to make a living.

We'll begin by diving deep into the digital nomad lifestyle. Then, we'll unlock the secrets to becoming a successful TripLeader: **from planning to enrich co-working trips, promoting them effectively, and managing sales, to handling the unexpected with** ease. **We'll discuss choosing perfect destinations, creating memorable experiences, and tackling the logistical challenges that accompany such adventures.**

Our aim is not just to inspire, but to provide you with a practical, comprehensive understanding of this lifestyle. This guide is designed to save you time, energy, and resources by providing a proven framework to plan, organize, and execute successful co-working trips.

The exciting part? You can embark on this journey without giving up your primary job or business. This guide offers you a fun and rewarding way to supplement your income, meet intriguing people, and feed your wanderlust.

Whether you're a seasoned traveler, a remote work rookie, or someone seeking a break from the mundane 9-5 grind, this guide is your passport to a lifestyle brimming with adventure, freedom, and fulfillment.

Let's get ready for a journey filled with excitement, personal growth, challenges, and boundless opportunities. Remember, each challenge is merely a stepping stone to new learning and growth.

By the end of this guide, don't be surprised if you're itching to book a one-way ticket to your first co-working trip adventure! Ready to start? Our first stop: exploring the captivating life of a Digital Nomad. **Let's set sail, shall we?**

CHAPTER 2

Journey into the Nomadic Lifestyle: Nico's Personal Experience

2.1 Meet Your Guide, Nico

Now, you might be wondering, "Who's this person babbling about getting paid to travel and sipping lattés in Paris?" Fair question. Let me introduce myself.

Greetings, fellow wanderers! It's about time you meet the spirit behind this guide.

I'm **Nico**, a genuine lover of life, people, and meaningful connections, hailing from the southern charm of Naples, Italy. Yes, the birthplace of the real pizza! But my story is more than just the flavorful and vibrant vibes of my hometown. It's a narrative of transformation, resilience, and the relentless pursuit of happiness.

I have always been an ambitious individual, embracing the digital world as a freelancer and running my own online business. My work typically spanned from morning till evening, the so-called traditional 9-6 grind. But it wasn't confined within the four walls of an office. Rather, it was an expansive adventure, my curiosity being the compass.

However, a few years back, a storm of life-altering events disrupted my usual rhythm. It was a tough period that reminded me of life's fleeting nature and its unpredictable twists and turns. It was a rough wake-up call, an echoing whisper in my ear that said: **"TODAY YOU ARE HERE, TOMORROW YOU DON'T KNOW."**

With that realization, my world seemed to be in a haze, making me question my purpose and direction. But in these moments of confusion, I found clarity in my memories of an experience that had profoundly shaped me—my Erasmus trip to **Malaga** in Spain.

This journey ignited a passionate love for diversity, for the unexplored, and the thrillingly unfamiliar. I immersed myself in different cultures, people, languages, and food. It was a transformative time that encouraged me to show my authentic self, helping me discover the essence of who I really am.

That trip was a spark that fueled my love for the new and exciting, making each day unique and thrilling. With a fresh perspective and a strong desire to break away from the conventional, I took a sabbatical from my routine and embraced the life of a digital nomad. I began to work remotely, feeling the sand between my toes and the soothing lull of the sea as my backdrop.

This nomadic lifestyle was an awakening. It made me more self-aware and confident, inspiring me to dedicate my life to what truly brings me joy—traveling, discovering, and filling my life with happy, memorable moments.

And so, I became a TripLeader, a role that allowed me to plan and lead trips for people seeking an escape from their monotonous life. Every trip I led made me stronger, wiser, and more determined to achieve whatever I set my heart on.

Now, my life is about seizing every day to create as many moments of joy as possible. It's about breaking free from "traditional structures" and using my time to truly **LIVE**! And through this guide, I hope to share this beautiful journey with you. **Let's turn travel into profit, together!**

2.2 An Unexpected Twist

Life has a funny way of making us rethink our paths, especially when we least expect it. It's funny how a tornado can whirl into your life, rip away the structures you've built, and leave you questioning everything you once knew as certainty. Well, I'm Nico, and **I'd like to tell you about the tornado that swept through my life.**

I was deeply immersed in my work as a digital marketing manager, managing a thriving online business, and working as a freelancer. The digital realm was my comfort zone, a place where I could leverage my skills and fuel my passion. But like a gentle breeze that suddenly turns into a powerful gust, my life took an unexpected turn.

I had always been a self-starter, driven by a spirit of entrepreneurship, building my own projects from the ground up. My days were filled with work, every single day, mornings, afternoons, and nights.

Then one day, I felt the world around me start to blur. I felt as though I was standing at a crossroads with signs pointing in different directions, each beckoning me into the unknown. All I knew was that I had to break free from the rigid patterns of my life.

You might imagine that at this point, I spontaneously landed on a sun-soaked beach in **Malaga**, sipping sangria with my laptop at my side, while the sound of the waves formed the perfect symphony of my newfound freedom. Well, the truth is, the transition was not quite as seamless, and the path to this idyllic picture was not straight. But we'll get to that. Let's go back a bit to where this all started.

2.3 The Maiden Voyage

As I'm typing these words, I find myself nestled in the historic charm of Maastricht, the Netherlands. The aroma of fresh stroopwafel lingers in the air, and the echo of shared laughter from an epic road trip with a recently made friend and fellow TripMate reverberates in my mind. We've journeyed through serpentine roads, marveled at breathtaking landscapes, and discovered hidden gems in these cobblestone-lined streets.

But let's journey back in time a bit. When I first stepped into the world of digital nomadism, it wasn't the exotic allure of Marrakech or the cultural vibrancy of Bangkok that called to me. Instead, I found my baptism by fire in the heart of the Mediterranean - **Sicily**.

Embarking on this journey with seven other remote workers, the rustic charm of Sicily served as our playground. This wasn't your run-of-the-mill vacation; it was a grand experiment in co-living, co-working, and embracing the digital nomad lifestyle. Everything was going smoothly until, one day, the sunny Sicilian skies turned dark.

In the second week, we were caught in the grip of one of the most severe storms in Sicily's history. Our cozy villa was suddenly transformed into an island surrounded by a sea of water. Food supplies dwindled, and the serenity of our remote work getaway seemed a distant memory.

Yet, in the midst of this adversity, something remarkable happened. We came together as a team, adapting and innovating to navigate the challenges thrown our way. The storm outside was ferocious, but inside, there was warmth, camaraderie, and a whole lot of problem-solving.

What could have been a disastrous experience turned into a treasured memory. It was a testament to our resilience, our shared **sense of community**, and the unyielding human spirit to adapt and thrive in the face of adversity. The echoes of that stormy week in Sicily continue to resonate in our hearts, a nostalgic symphony that we, the first group/family, still reminisce about years later.

That trip was a turning point for me. It highlighted the power of community, the thrill of adapting to the unexpected, and the rewarding challenge of leading a group through thick and thin. **It was my first taste of being a TripLeader, and from that moment on, I was hooked.**

From there, my journey took me to Malaga, Napoli, Crete, Cyprus … and beyond the European continent, **Marrakech**, with its vibrant colors and bustling souks. Amidst the heady mix of fragrant spices, vivid tapestries, and the soulful Adhan echoing through the city, I felt an affirming sense of freedom and a conviction that I chose the right path. I will never forget one particularly profound moment etched in my memory: <u>me starring at the stars in the middle of the Sahara desert by night while on a Co-Working trip.</u> The cool sand was under my feet, and the calm desert wind was my lullaby. At that moment, I felt a rush of pure joy that made my heart sing… **I was alive!**

The vast desert and the endless sky were no longer daunting, but filled with the promise of adventure and a life of unscripted joy. Every trip I lead is inspired by that unforgettable night. **My goal?** *To give others the chance to experience the thrill of being alive, of connecting, and of discovering that the world is an endless playground of exciting adventures.*

2.4 Becoming a TripLeader: Challenges, Triumphs, and Lessons

This newfound sense of liberation came with its fair share of challenges, of course. There were times when I felt out of my depth, when I questioned my choices, and when I missed the predictability of my old life.

But, you know what? Each challenge was a lesson in disguise. Each stumbling block, an opportunity to grow. With every new location, I learned to adapt, negotiate, immerse myself in different cultures, and ultimately, flourish.

From managing lost luggage to navigating language barriers, from resolving last-minute itinerary changes to dealing with a flat tire in the middle of nowhere, I've seen it all. **But the rewards of this lifestyle make every challenge worth it.**

Imagine being in a small town in Spain, sharing an authentic paella with a group of strangers who, over the course of the trip, have become more like a family. Or the joy of witnessing the wonder in your TripMates' eyes as they experience new cultures and landscapes.

Being a **TripLeader** is about more than just organizing trips. It's about building connections, creating memorable experiences, and turning a diverse group of strangers into a tight-knit community.

So, here we are, at the end of Chapter two. We've just begun to scratch the surface of what being a TripLeader entails. As we move forward, I'll share the nitty-gritty of planning and executing successful co-working trips.

In the next chapter, we delve into the heart of the matter: understanding Co-working trips.

Stay tuned, fellow adventurers! **This journey is just getting started.**

CHAPTER 3

UNDERSTANDING CO-WORKING TRIPS

3.1 The Who, What, and Where of Co-Working Trips

Co-working trips—two words that have become a mantra for countless digital nomads worldwide. But what do these words truly encapsulate? Picture a tranquil beach setting with the rhythmic sound of the ocean in the background, a cooling drink by your side, your fingers dancing on your laptop keyboard. This idyllic vision, dear reader, is a glimpse into the world of co-working trips.

Co-working trips bring together work and leisure, intertwining them in a beautiful dance that makes life more exciting and fulfilling. They allow individuals, typically freelancers, entrepreneurs, or remote workers, to work and network in some of the world's most inspiring, often sun-drenched locations for periods ranging from a week to a month. It's like your typical coffee break at the office, but instead of trading stories about the weather, you're sharing tales of your latest adventure in an unexplored city.

A co-working trip is not just a vacation, it's an immersive experience designed to foster personal and professional growth. They help you break free from the confines of conventional workspaces and tap into a new source of inspiration. Each trip is an opportunity to broaden your horizons and encounter people from various cultures and walks of life.

Here are a few highlights of a co-working trip experience:

- **Community Building:** Co-working trips offer a unique opportunity to immerse yourself in a community of like-minded individuals. You'll form connections with an array of people from diverse backgrounds who share your zest for exploration and remote work. This shared experience will help you build genuine, lasting relationships, exchange ideas, and establish a supportive network that enriches your personal and professional life.

- **Boosting Productivity:** Working remotely can sometimes feel isolating, but on a co-working trip, you'll be surrounded by motivated, ambitious individuals. Working in this collective, dynamic environment can significantly enhance your productivity, encouraging you to achieve more and tap into your creative potential.

- **Self-discovery & Growth:** Co-working trips offer much more than a change of scenery. They provide an environment conducive to personal and professional growth. As you learn from others, share your experiences, and support each other's dreams, you'll realize that your potential knows no bounds. They are a platform for self-discovery, helping you see the world and yourself through a new lens.

A coworking trip has the power to transform your life. As a TripLeader, I've witnessed many people surmount their personal hurdles through these journeys. The change in perspective they provide often leads to profound personal and professional growth. Remember, the world is out there, ready for you to explore. Embrace the unknown, feel the thrill of discovery, and let a co-working trip shape your life as a digital nomad and beyond.

In the words of Anthony Bourdain, "Travel isn't always pretty. It isn't always comfortable. Sometimes it hurts, it even breaks your heart. But that's okay. The journey changes you; it should change you... You take something with you. Hopefully, you leave something good behind."

3.2 The Rainbow of Co-Working Trips

Think of co-working trips as a rainbow, each color representing a unique blend of experiences catering to **different passions and interests**. Just as a seasoned traveler's passport boasts a medley of stamps from all corners of the globe, the world of co-working trips is brimming with thrilling options that cater to the adventurer, the connoisseur, the yogi, and everyone in between.

Picture yourself as an adventure enthusiast, **scaling** the Atlas Mountains with a band of fellow digital nomads, exchanging coding tips amidst the echoes of the wilderness. Or imagine unwinding with a yoga session on a tranquil Balinese beach, your workday concluding with the golden sunset and the rhythmic lullaby of the waves.

For the gastronomes among you, envision a **culinary tour** in the heart of Sicily, where you can satisfy your palate with local delicacies while brainstorming your latest project. Or perhaps you're a wine enthusiast; then picture a coworking trip set in the rolling vineyards of Bordeaux, discussing market strategies over **wine-tasting** sessions.

If **cycling** is your passion, imagine whizzing past picturesque landscapes in the Netherlands with a group of like-minded nomads, sharing ideas over the shared adrenaline rush. Every pit stop becomes an opportunity for a quick sync-up or a brainstorming session.

The beauty of co-working trips lies in their flexibility and diversity. There's something for every taste, every interest. Whether you're a thrill-seeker, a tranquility lover, a foodie, or a passionate hobbyist, there's a co-working trip out there that's just your shade of the rainbow.

So, grab your laptop, pack your bags, and prepare for a roller-coaster ride of work, leisure, and exploration. Get ready to dip your toes into the colorful spectrum of co-working trips and discover the hue that best complements your digital nomad lifestyle.

There's a whole rainbow out there waiting for you to explore. In the words of Dr. Seuss, "*Oh, the places you'll go!*"

3.3 Beyond the Trend: The Longevity of These Adventures

Co-working trips aren't a fleeting trend or a flight of fancy. Instead, they are an <u>innovative blend of travel, work, and personal growth</u>, offering you a wealth of tangible benefits that can transform your professional journey and personal life.

First off, let's talk about flexibility. The concept of co-working trips redefines the conventional office setup, giving you the freedom to explore the world without compromising your career. Remember the days when you exhaust all your leave days for that one-week vacation, only to return to an intimidating pile of work? With co-working trips, you can say goodbye to those days.Imagine working on your presentation against the backdrop of a stunning sunset in Malaga, or dialing into those routine calls as you traverse the mountainous trails of Madeira. That's the kind of work-life balance co-working trips offer.

Next up is the international community that co-working trips invite you to be a part of. **This isn't just about sharing a workspace or a stable Wi-Fi connection.** It's about sharing adventures, experiences, and cultures. It's about engaging in exciting conversations, brainstorming sessions, and debates over dinner. You might start your co-working trip with a bunch of strangers, but by the end of it, you'll likely leave with a new circle of lifelong friends and a wider professional network.

Lastly, co-working trips push you out of **your comfort zone**, challenging you to embrace and adapt to new cultures, learn new languages, and navigate the uncharted waters of unfamiliar territories. Each destination is a classroom in disguise, teaching lessons in resilience, adaptability, and personal growth. You'll find that the learning curve on a co-working trip is steep but incredibly rewarding.

In short, co-working trips are not just a travel trend. **They are a lifestyle choice, a professional enhancement, and a catalyst for personal growth.** They invite you to explore the world, expand your horizons, and enrich your life with unforgettable experiences and lasting connections. So, are you ready to rewrite your work life?

Stay tuned for the next chapter, where we'll dive into the nitty-gritty of transitioning from traditional employment to remote work, as well as explore the myriad of opportunities this lifestyle offers.

Buckle up, because our adventure into the world of co-working trips is just getting started!

CHAPTER 4

EMBARKING ON YOUR REMOTE WORK JOURNEY

Hello, dear reader! As we delve into the fourth chapter of our journey together, we're about to explore an exciting and transformative phase - **transitioning to remote work**. Are you ready to embark on this thrilling adventure? Well, then, let's dive in!

4.1 Making the Leap: Transitioning from Traditional to Remote Work

The decision to ditch my traditional job, pack up my bags, and dive headfirst into the digital nomad lifestyle was a leap into the unknown. But, having navigated those uncharted waters, I can tell you that not only is this transition achievable, but it's also one of the best professional decisions I've ever made. Now, let me share some insights to help you transition from your current job into the flexible, location-independent world of remote work.

Reassess Your Current Position: The initial step involves taking a good look at your current role. Can your job tasks be performed remotely? In today's digital age, many companies are opening up to the idea of remote work, given its proven benefits for both employee well-being and productivity. If your role is one that can be accomplished effectively from anywhere globally, it's worth exploring the possibility of transitioning it into a remote one.

Craft Your Proposal: This isn't about simply walking into your boss's office and asking to work remotely. Instead, it's about presenting a well-thought-out proposal that addresses potential concerns and demonstrates the benefits. Begin by doing your research - gather data about remote work, cite studies that show its effectiveness, and perhaps offer examples of similar roles or businesses that have successfully adopted remote work. Additionally, propose a trial period to illustrate your ability to maintain (or even increase) productivity while working remotely.

Upskill: The world of remote work, while liberating, requires you to stay abreast of various tools and technologies. Equip yourself with proficiency in essential remote work tools, like video conferencing platforms such as Zoom, team communication tools like Slack, and project management applications like Asana or Trello. Familiarize yourself with collaborative platforms like Google Workspace. Continuous learning is key in the evolving landscape of remote work.

Financial Planning: Embarking on a digital nomad lifestyle entails ensuring that you have a sturdy financial safety net. It's advisable to have an emergency fund that covers at least three to six months of your living expenses. This fund provides the financial security you need during the transition period and offers peace of mind as you explore the exciting world of remote work and travel.

4.2 The Wide World of Remote Work Opportunities

The digital world has flung open its doors wide to a myriad of remote work opportunities. It's like a candy shop out there, and you, my friend, have got the golden ticket! So, whether you're a freelancer, a consultant, a remote employee, or a budding entrepreneur, brace yourself for the ride of a lifetime.

Freelancing: Step into the thriving universe of freelancing, where you can wear many hats. From coding wizards and design virtuosos to pen-wielding wordsmiths and social media mavens, freelancing offers a vibrant array of opportunities. And the best part? Websites like Upwork, Freelancer, Fiverr, and even niche platforms like 99Designs (for designers), ProBlogger (for writers), and Toptal (for top 3% freelance talent) serve as bustling marketplaces teeming with clients who need your expertise.

Consulting: Fancy yourself a guru in your field? Well, consulting might just be your golden goose. As a consultant, you can provide valuable advice to businesses eager to elevate their performance. Here's a quick tip to get started: Begin by defining your niche and setting up a professional website showcasing your experience and services. Leverage LinkedIn to connect with potential clients and consider writing industry-specific articles to establish yourself as a thought leader in your domain.

Remote Employee: Welcome to the 21st century, where businesses are not only warming up to remote work, but they're also actively seeking remote employees! Numerous platforms like Remote.co, WeWorkRemotely, and FlexJobs curate an extensive list of remote job opportunities spanning various fields. So whether you're an engineer, marketer, HR professional, or anything in between, your dream remote job could just be a click away.

Entrepreneurship: Got a business idea that keeps you up at night? As a digital nomad, you can harness the power of the internet to set up and run a business from practically anywhere in the world. All you need is a trusty laptop, a solid internet connection, a sprinkle of tenacity, and a generous helping of dedication.

Next, let's take a peek at some stellar platforms for **hunting high-quality remote jobs**. These websites have been my trusty companions on my digital nomad journey, and I'm confident they'll serve you just as well.

Dynamite Jobs: is like the secret menu at your favorite diner, offering a unique salary filter to help you save time and avoid job listings that don't meet your expectations. The site is incredibly user-friendly and covers a broad range of job categories. And guess what? It's absolutely free!

FlexJobs: Think of FlexJobs as your personal remote job sommelier, offering a curated selection of remote, freelance, and flexible jobs across various career stages. The jobs and companies listed are meticulously vetted for quality. FlexJobs does charge a <u>membership fee</u>, but it's a small price to pay for such a treasure trove of opportunities.

Indeed: Indeed is like the bustling job market square of the digital world, with opportunities spanning every industry and job type. It's super easy to find relevant jobs, and you can even store your resume on the site for lightning-fast applications. The best part? <u>It's completely free</u>!

Remote.co: The brainchild of FlexJobs' founder, Sara Sutton, Remote.co is a dedicated hub for remote jobs. It boasts a wealth of job listings across various fields and, bonus, <u>it's free</u>, and most listings provide expected salary information!

RemoteOK: Picture RemoteOK as your personal job concierge. Its impressive search filters allow you to find jobs based on location, salary, and even specific employer benefits.

4.3 Landing Your First Remote Work Opportunity

Just as a pirate rejoices in unearthing buried treasure, snagging your first remote work opportunity is nothing short of an adrenaline rush. Aye, me hearties! <u>Here are a few pointers to get you sailing towards that horizon.</u>

Online Portfolio: Think of your online portfolio as the storefront of your brand, where you get to flaunt your skills, experience, and projects like a proud peacock. Add a dash of creativity, stir in some personality, and voila, you have a captivating portfolio. Don't forget to include clear contact information and client testimonials, if any. Websites like Behance, Dribbble, Tilda or even a personal Wordpress site can serve as a great platform for your portfolio.

Remote Job Applications: Crafting remote job applications is a fine art. Start with a cover letter that shines brighter than a lighthouse in a stormy sea. Accentuate your remote work skills, highlight your independence, and underline your ability to juggle different time zones (if applicable). Remember, each application should be tailored to the job description, so resist the temptation to use a generic cover letter. A personal touch goes a long way!

Networking: Networking is like casting a wide net to catch that elusive golden fish. Attend virtual industry events, webinars, and meetups like they're happening right in your living room (which they likely are!). Make **LinkedIn** your trusty sidekick:

- <u>Private Clients</u>: Join **LinkedIn groups** relevant to your industry and actively engage in discussions. This not only helps build your credibility but also increases your visibility to potential clients. Consider using LinkedIn automation tools to expand your network but remember, automation doesn't replace authenticity. Always aim for personalized outreach.

- <u>Job Opportunities:</u> Amp up your **LinkedIn profile** to make it a head-turner. Use keywords related to your industry in your headline and summary, and ensure your experience section is up-to-date and robust. A polished LinkedIn profile can be like a beacon to job recruiters.

Venturing onto the remote work plank may push you out of your comfort zone, but oh, the view from out there is spectacular. As they say, every journey of a thousand miles begins with a single step (or in our case, a click!). So, are you ready to embark on this thrilling voyage?

Let's set sail!

CHAPTER 5

ESSENTIAL SKILLS AND EQUIPMENT FOR A SUCCESSFUL TRIP LEADER

Alright folks, grab your pens, notebooks, iPads, or whatever you use for note-taking because we're about to dive into the nuts and bolts of being a Pro Trip Leader. Now, I could sit here and tell you it's all rainbows and butterflies, but hey, that's not my style! Let's get real and strip it down to the essentials.

5.1 Technical Skills

First off, **Internet Savviness** Let's face it, we live in the digital age. You might be heading off into the wild, but you aren't going completely off-grid. Unless you have some secret WiFi connection in the middle of the Amazon rainforest that I don't know about, in which case, do share! Being comfortable navigating the web is crucial.

Knowing your way around social media platforms, online booking sites, and travel apps isn't just a luxury, it's a necessity. Sure, you could ask a 5-year-old, they're practically born with this knowledge these days, but that's not quite the image of a competent TripLeader now, is it?

Next, **Basic Graphic Design** Now, I know you're probably thinking, "Oh, great, as if I didn't have enough to worry about." Fear not! I'm not asking you to be the next Da Vinci. Tools like Canva make it as easy as pie, just watch a few tutorials on YouTube and voila! You're going to need this to create some 'wow' factor for your social media content and trip promotional materials.

Finally, **Photography Skills.** No, you don't have to take Vogue-worthy shots, but let's not kid ourselves, those Instagrammable moments aren't going to capture themselves. A good quality image can speak volumes about your trips and lure in those hesitant TripMates.

5.2 Interpersonal Skills

Let's not mince words here; you can't do without interpersonal skills if you're dreaming of becoming a top-notch Trip Leader. Interpersonal skills are the secret sauce that turns a "meh" trip into a "wow, that was unforgettable!" trip. So, buckle up, and let's dive in.

Communication Skills

Clear communication is absolutely non-negotiable. We're not talking Morse code or smoke signals here, my friends. We're talking about your ability to convey all the necessary information to your group in a way they can easily understand. From the nitty-gritty details of the itinerary to spontaneous changes (because life happens, even on the road), you need to keep your team updated. And let's not forget those language barriers, cultural sensitivities, or even the occasional feud between TripMates.

Your communication skills are the bridge that spans all those chasms, keeping your group in sync and in high spirits.

Empathy and Patience

Empathy and patience are what differentiate a Trip Leader from a Trip Dictator. **No two travelers are the same.** You'll be dealing with all sorts of personalities, comfort zones, and travel experiences. You'll need to be able to put yourself in their shoes, to understand and respect their individual needs and limitations. And trust me, this empathy will be appreciated. As for patience, well, let's just say there will be times when your TripMates test yours to the limits. Missed flights, lost items, last-minute changes of plans, or just an off day — these things happen.

A little patience goes a long way in keeping the trip enjoyable for everyone.

Problem-Solving Skills

Stuff happens, it's inevitable. Even with the best-laid plans, there will be times when things go sideways. This is where your

problem-solving skills come into play. Missed that bus to the next city? No worries, you'll find another route. Attraction closed for renovation? You know another equally exciting place. You're not just solving problems; you're actively creating a positive experience for your TripMates. The key here is to stay calm and think on your feet.

The quicker and smoother you can manage these hiccups, the less they'll impact the overall trip experience.

Leadership Skills

As a Trip Leader, you are the captain of the ship. This doesn't mean you rule with an iron fist, but rather that you are a guiding light, a point of stability, and yes, sometimes even a cheerleader. You need to lead by example, be it respecting local customs, adhering to schedules, or just keeping the energy levels high. You need to be there for your TripMates, to listen, to advise, to help. It's about fostering a sense of community, where everyone feels welcome and a part of the journey. Remember, the journey is as much about the people as it is about the places.

Make sure every TripMate feels valued, heard, and included, and you'll have yourself an unforgettable adventure!

5.3 Essential Equipment for Content Creation and Management

Now, let's talk gear. You're like a digital knight, and every knight needs his armor and sword.

Your Laptop. This isn't just a piece of machinery, it's your office, your planner, your connection to the world. Make sure it's reliable, lightweight, and with a decent battery life. Two laptop examples that can be perfect for a digital nomad:

1. **Dell XPS 15**: This is a powerful laptop with an impressive display. It's great for content creation tasks like video editing or graphic design. Plus, it's compact and lightweight, making it a good fit for digital nomads.

2. **MacBook Pro 13**: Known for its superior build quality and excellent performance, the MacBook Pro 13 is a favorite among many digital nomads. The high-resolution Retina display is great for any visual work, and the machine is powerful enough to handle most tasks with ease.

A Smartphone with a Good Camera. Let's be honest, lugging around a bulky DSLR isn't always practical. A smartphone with a good camera is a must. It's not just for snapping pics but also for keeping up with emails, social media, and yes, the occasional map when you inevitably get lost.

Reliable Internet Connection. Remember when I mentioned we're not going off-grid? This is why. Whether it's a local SIM card or a portable WiFi device (80 - 250€), ensure you're always connected.

A Good Backpack. This isn't just a bag; it's your home. Examples of good backpacks:

1. **Osprey Farpoint 40 Travel Backpack**: This backpack is perfect for digital nomads. It's durable, spacious, and has a lockable laptop compartment for added security. Plus, it's carry-on size, which makes traveling between destinations a breeze.

2. **Nomatic Travel Bag**: Nomatic's backpack is designed for a 3-7 day trip. It features a patented strap system that allows you to go from duffel to backpack carry, multiple compartments for shoes, water bottles, and valuables, and it also has a special laptop pocket.

But remember, everything depends on your preferences and needs, howeve, these are some of the best options on the market up to date.

CHAPTER 6

TripLeader Academy: Your Passport to Success

Imagine having the world as your classroom, the globe-trotting experts as your teachers, and the thrilling pursuit of passion-fueled adventures as your syllabus. Welcome to the **TripLeader Academy!**

At the heart of the TripLeader Academy lies a relentless commitment to transform you into a master TripLeader. This isn't your average, run-of-the-mill training program. No, it's a powerhouse of resources designed meticulously to help you unlock your fullest potential, lead unforgettable trips, and explore new destinations without sacrificing your job/business.

As a part of the TripLeader Academy, you aren't just handed a rulebook; you're equipped with an arsenal of **tools, channels, platforms, tips,** and **tricks** tailored to elevate your trip leading game.

The training steers you beyond the usual to help you kindle your passion, build a vibrant community, and map out extraordinary adventures around the globe.

What's more, the academy promises a personal touch, providing you with one-on-one guidance. It's like having a seasoned mentor walk alongside you, celebrating your triumphs, and helping you navigate the challenges.

And the benefits? They're as vast as the ocean! From gaining access to an international network of travel enthusiasts to earning while you explore, the perks of becoming a TripLeader are plenty.

Are you ready to swap the mundane for the magical? Dive in and let the TripLeader Academy be your passport to a world of endless possibilities.

6.1 Unparalleled Resources and Support

At the TripLeader Academy, we ensure you're never navigating your journey alone. We've got a treasure chest of resources at your disposal round the clock. From video tutorials and detailed guides to interactive webinars, we've got you covered on all things trip leading. Whether you're planning your trip, in the thick of the adventure, or wrapping up after a successful journey, we have insights and instructions ready for you.

Plus, we have a buzzing **community** of TripLeaders from around the world, ready to share their experiences and wisdom. The Academy also offers continuous support from our dedicated team, who are always ready to dive into action should you need any assistance.

6.2 Personalized Coaching Structure

Let's introduce you to the backbone of our Academy - **our personalized coaching structure.** It's like having a seasoned mentor on speed dial, guiding you through every step of your trip leading journey.

Led by yours truly, Nico, the founder of TripLeader Academy, the coaching program is a sequence of intimate and insightful sessions, tailor-made to set you up for success.

Here's a quick overview:

- **The "Hello" Call**: Think of this as your warm-up session, where you get a taste of what lies ahead in your trip leading journey. This brief interaction is just enough to whet your appetite for the adventure to come.

- **The Blueprint Session**: This is where we start turning your dreams into reality. Together, we'll brainstorm trip destinations, sketch out the skills you can bring to the table, and dive into the nitty-gritty of planning your trip.

- **The Check-In Calls:** Your journey doesn't end with planning; we're with you every step of the way. During these sessions, we'll fine-tune your trip and personalized promotion strategies, answer your burning questions, and ensure your progress is on track.

- **The Wrap-Up Call:** All good things come to an end, and so does your preparation stage. In this session, we'll address any last-minute queries you might have and make sure you're ready to take the world by storm.

And the cherry on top? <u>You can book additional 1-on-1 calls</u> with me whenever you need a little extra guidance. With this bespoke support, you're never alone in your journey. You get the help you need, exactly when you need it. Now that's what we call personalized coaching!

6.3 Taking it Forward

The TripLeader Academy isn't just about preparing you for your first trip. We want to help you grow even beyond your first successful journey. We continue to support you by hosting your trips on our platforms, thus enabling you to reach a larger audience.

Ready for a lifelong journey of discovery? The TripLeader Academy supports you beyond your first trip, ensuring your continuous growth and success in the world of travel.

Choose your pathway:

- **Self-Learner Route**: Explore our comprehensive online course at www.tripleaderacademy.com. Delve into in-depth video content, engaging exercises, and a plethora of resources tailored for your trip-leading journey.

- **Personalized Coach Route**: Get one-on-one mentorship with our founder, Nico, for bespoke advice, guidance tailored to your specific needs, personalized support, exclusive access to travel platforms we are in partnership with, and your personal landing page.

As an exclusive offer for our ebook readers, enjoy a special discount on both pathways. Simply mention that you've read our ebook when contacting us. Let's get started on this thrilling journey! Find our contact details on www.tripleaderacademy.com.

CHAPTER 7

PLANNING AND ORGANIZING YOUR FIRST CO-WORKING TRIP

Embarking on a co-working expedition is a one-of-a-kind adventure that combines work, exploration, and the joy of communal living for at least a week. Unlike a traditional guided tour, a co-working trip thrives on the synergistic blend of its participants. Here's a deep dive into the elements you must consider when planning this unique expedition.

7.1 How to choose the ideal destination

Your co-working adventure is a reflection of your wanderlust. This liberty allows you to tailor your journey to any place that sparks your interest. While virtually any location could host a co-working trip, certain spots often strike a chord with digital nomads. The perfect mix of climate and culture usually entails warm beachfront cities bursting with vibrant local traditions.

If you're planning a return trip to a <u>previously visited location,</u> that's a gold mine! Your insider knowledge of local hotspots and dining treasures will be invaluable. Still unsure about where to set your co-working adventure? Leverage the power of the internet. Search for 'top destinations for remote workers' or immerse yourself in digital nomad communities to learn about their preferred locations. **Nomadlist** is a great resource to get started.

Google's Destination Insights is another valuable tool that provides a wealth of data on trending locations for travelers. Classic cities for co-working trips include Fuerteventura, Tenerife, Rome, Lisbon, Bali, Chiang Mai, Madeira, Athens, Budapest, and Mexico City.

7.2 The Ideal Living Space

A successful co-working trip hinges on the right accommodation. We need a dwelling that not only promotes productivity but also serves as a haven for relaxation. Look for **spacious villas or apartments** within the same building that offer:

- 3 to 5 bedrooms (single or shared rooms are preferable)

- 2 to 5 bathrooms

- Dedicated workstations in each room (extra credit for these!)

- Reliable and high-speed Wi-Fi connectivity (verified speed test results)

- Outdoor spaces like gardens or balconies

Additional amenities can amplify the charm of the house, such as a BBQ setup, swimming pool, jacuzzi, gym, billiards/table tennis, and **a breathtaking view**. Ensure that everyone has ample space for their calls or work without disturbing others. A location close to the city center or public transportation is a plus; otherwise, consider renting a car (to share with your Tripmates).

7.3 Housing Platforms Worth Bookmarking

The most suitable platform for finding accommodations can vary based on your destination. Here are some you might want to try:

- Airbnb (Excellent for co-working villas)

- Google Map (Direct rentals from the owner or agency)

- Booking.com (Villas or flats)

- Housinganywhere.com

- FB groups (e.g., Malaga house renting, Flats in Greece)

- TripAdvisor

- Flatio.com

- Pisos.com

- Fotocasa.es (Spain)

Don't forget to use a **VPN** to access local offers.

7.4 Crafting the Perfect Itinerary

When crafting the perfect itinerary for your co-working trip, remember it's about striking a **balance between work and play.** As such, your itinerary doesn't need to be chock-full of sightseeing activities. The key is to allow your fellow trip mates to relax, work, and explore during their free time.

Plan for day trips and short excursions that will enrich your travel experience without overwhelming the group. For example, on a previous co-working trip to Malaga, we visited five key stops including Sevilla, Granada, and Nerja, with a couple of additional afternoon or evening destinations within easy reach.

Wondering where to find unique experiences or activities for your co-working trip? Here are a few resources to consider:

- Airbnb Experiences

- TripAdvisor

- GetYourGuide.com

- Thecrazytourist.com

- Bookmundi.com

- Viator.com

- Google Search (e.g. "What to do in Crete in 2 days?")

Remember, a co-working trip isn't just about sightseeing. Fun activities like surfing, scuba diving, horse riding, and more can be the main themes of your trip. It's about finding a balance that suits your group and creates lasting memories.

7.5 How to Make the Final Price

Calculating the final price for a co-working trip is typically straightforward, with the main components being accommodation and your **TripLeader fee.** Here's a suggested breakdown:

1. **Accommodation**: Consider a two-week stay in either a shared or private bedroom.

2. **Transportation**: If you plan to rent a car, decide whether you want to include this in the final price or split it with your TripMates later using apps such as Splitwise

3. **Your Expenses**: Account for your flight costs, daily expenses during the stay, food costs, car rental costs, activities, etc.

4. **Buffer**: Include a 10% buffer to cover unexpected costs.

5. **Your Fee**: Determine your fee based on the effort you put into planning the trip and how much you plan to earn.

For a typical co-working trip, the price usually ranges from 550€ to 950€ per TripMate for a shared or private room.

7.6 Tips for a Stellar Co-Working Trip

1. **Choose the right house:** Look for spacious and comfortable accommodations with dedicated common workspaces and high-speed Wi-Fi. Additional amenities like a pool, jacuzzi, BBQ area, games, or a gym can be bonuses.

2. **Set clear expectations**: Your trip description should accurately reflect what your TripMates can expect from the trip. Picture them while being on your upcoming experience.

3. **Consider a pool**: A pool can be a selling point, especially for trips to warmer climates.

4. **Choose an interesting location**: A location that offers unique sights and relaxation spots can influence the success of your co-working trip.

5. **Create a balanced itinerary**: Co-working trips should maintain a balance between work and leisure. Don't overcrowd the itinerary.

Finally, remember that a co-working trip is about making lifelong connections and shared memories with a group of flexible and open-minded professionals.

7.7 Enriching Activities and Workshops for a Co-Working Trip

Transform your co-working trips into a rich tapestry of experiences with a mix of engaging activities and workshops that foster camaraderie, creativity, and fun. Let's dive in.

1. **Personal Introductions**: What better way to break the ice than by sharing personal stories? By sharing past travel experiences, professional backgrounds, and memorable travel moments, group members can bond and find common ground. It's a fantastic way to create an atmosphere of trust, openness, and mutual understanding from the outset.

2. **Morning Fitness Fun**: Wake up with a splash of energy! Whether it's yoga on the beach, a brisk morning hike, or a friendly game of Frisbee, incorporating fitness activities can keep everyone feeling fresh and invigorated. Plus, it's a great way to create shared memories and stories.

3. **Tic Tac Toe Icebreaker:** Everyone has a unique passion or hobby that defines them. By sharing these interests, participants can learn about each other in a fun and informal way. The element of surprise often leads to laughter and connections that endure beyond the trip.

4. **Show & Tell Evenings:** Give everyone a chance to share something they're passionate about. Whether it's a magic trick, a favorite book, or a cooking lesson, these evenings

allow for personal expression, respect for diversity, and the building of a rich, multi-faceted group dynamic.

5. **Sound Healing Sessions:** Unleash the transformative power of sound for personal growth and relaxation. These sessions, whether guided by a local expert or a willing group member, can provide a shared spiritual experience that brings everyone closer together.

6. **Group Meditation:** Lead a meditation session in a serene spot. This shared journey into tranquility can enhance focus, reduce stress, and promote a harmonious group vibe.

7. **Adventure Challenges:** Nothing says team-building quite like overcoming challenges together. Be it a local scavenger hunt, an impromptu soccer match with locals, or even a 'survival' cooking challenge, the adrenaline rush and shared laughter will strengthen bonds like nothing else.

8. **Karaoke Night**: Embrace the silliness and let everyone unleash their inner pop star! Karaoke is a hilarious and fun way to encourage everyone to let loose and enjoy themselves. Who knows, you might discover some hidden talents!

Co-working trips are not just about work or sightseeing. **They're about shared experiences, laughter, and growth**. Strike the right balance, and your co-working trip can truly become an unforgettable adventure.

Remember: *the key is to be flexible, creative, and inclusive when planning these activities.*

CHAPTER 8

Marketing Strategies for Your Co-Working Trip

A voyage without voyagers amounts to naught - such is the essence of a co-working trip. Therefore, the role of marketing becomes indispensable. This chapter endeavors to delve into the various **tactics** and **strategies** you can utilize to ensure your co-working trip is a sell-out.

8.1 Comprehensive Guide to Marketing Your Trip

Marketing your co-working trip starts with defining your **unique selling proposition (USP)**. Why should people choose your trip over others? Is it the destination, your leadership, the type of activities, the work-learning balance, or the overall vibe?

Once you've defined your USP, it's time to shout it from the rooftops. Use **storytelling** to make your marketing efforts compelling. Instead of just listing out features of your trip, tell a story. How will they feel when they join your trip? What transformations or experiences can they expect?

For instance, instead of saying "*We will be staying at a beautiful villa in Bali,*" try "*Imagine waking up in a gorgeous Balinese villa, starting your day with a refreshing dip in the pool, followed by a focused work session with the lush green rice fields as your backdrop. That's what our co-working trip offers you - a perfect blend of productivity and tranquility.*"

8.2 The Role of Organic Marketing

In today's digital age, organic marketing plays a crucial role in gaining visibility. Organic marketing refers to using **free tools and platforms** to build and engage with your audience. This includes SEO, social media, blogging, email marketing, and more.

The key to effective organic marketing is **consistency and engagement**. Regularly post valuable content on your chosen platforms. Engage with your audience through comments, messages, and emails. Remember, the goal of organic marketing is to build relationships and trust.

8.3 Proven Strategies to Get Fully Booked

Your ultimate aim is to fill up all the spots on your co-working trip. For this, you'll need to employ a multi-channel marketing approach. Here, we're going to break down **four major strategies** and how you can harness their power.

1. **Leverage Your Network:** It's often said, your network is your net worth, and it couldn't be truer in this case. So, your first port of call should be the people you already know - friends, family, colleagues, acquaintances, your gym buddies, even your dog's groomer!

2. Personal invitations go a long way. Share your excitement, tell them about the trip's USP, and extend an invitation. Even if they're unable to attend, they might know someone who would be interested. **Never underestimate the power of word-of-mouth!**

3. **Social Media:** Platforms like Instagram, LinkedIn, and Facebook aren't just for cute cat videos and funny memes, they're powerful marketing tools! So, get your social media hat on and start promoting your trip.

   - On **Instagram**, use high-quality visuals and captivating stories to make your posts engaging. LinkedIn is perfect for reaching out to professionals who might be interested in a co-working trip. Remember that tutorial on Canva? Use it to make your posts stand out!

   - On **Facebook**, in addition to your page, join relevant groups like "Digital Nomads Spain (Malaga)", "Remote Work & Travel", or "Entrepreneurs on the Move" and engage with their members. Remember, engagement isn't just about promoting your trip. Respond to comments, ask questions, and be a part of the conversation. This will increase your visibility and credibility.

4. **Email Marketing:** Harness the power of email marketing to create excitement and anticipation for your co-working trip. If you don't already have an email list, now is the time to start building one. There are several platforms available for this, including Mailchimp, SendinBlue, and ConvertKit, each offering a range of features to manage and segment your email lists.

To attract subscribers, offer a valuable freebie (also known as a 'lead magnet') in exchange for their email address. This could be an informative guide on co-working travel, a list of essential items for a co-working trip, or exclusive early access to your trip details. You can advertise these freebies on your website, social media channels, or even through paid ads.

Once you have a growing email list, the next step is to create an engaging email marketing campaign. This typically includes a series of emails designed to keep your audience informed and excited about your trip. Here's a simple roadmap:

- **The Introductory Email**: Introduce your upcoming co-working trip. Give a sneak peek into what it entails, whetting their appetite for more information.

- **The Itinerary Email:** Delve into the details. Unveil the itinerary, the destinations, workshops, and unique features of the trip.

- **Early Bird Offers**: Offer special prices or bonuses for those who sign up early. This creates incentive and adds a sense of urgency.

- **Exciting Updates:** Keep your audience in the loop with regular updates about the trip. This could include additions to the itinerary, fun facts about the destination, or profiles of confirmed attendees.

- **The Last Call:** Create a sense of urgency with "last few spots remaining" emails. This can spur indecisive subscribers into action.

Remember, the goal of email marketing is not just to sell but to build relationships. Keep the tone of your emails friendly and conversational. Let your passion for the trip shine through each email. It's not just about the information you're delivering; it's also about establishing trust, enthusiasm, and a sense of community around your co-working trip.

Remember, when it comes to marketing, one size does NOT fit all. Each of these strategies is like a recipe. Try it, tweak it, see what works for your unique flavor. Keep refining your tactics based on what gets you the best results. **Marketing is a marathon, not a**

sprint. So, keep going, keep testing, and most importantly, keep having fun!

8.4 Utilizing social media platforms for organic reach

In the age of digital marketing, social media is your most potent tool. Platforms like Instagram, Facebook, LinkedIn, and Twitter are fantastic for reaching out to potential trip-goers and for nurturing your existing community.

Let's delve deeper into the strategies for LinkedIn and Facebook, your powerhouses for professional networking and community building.

LinkedIn

LinkedIn is your **professional window** to the world. It's not just for job searching – it's a platform for fostering connections, sharing insights, and positioning yourself as a leader in your field. It's also the perfect platform to reach potential trip-goers who would be interested in a co-working trip.

1. **Automating LinkedIn Outreach:** Tools like Dux-Soup and Expandi offer automation services for LinkedIn outreach. These tools can automatically visit profiles, send connection requests, follow-up messages, and even endorse skills of potential connections based on the parameters you set. Remember, your goal is to build authentic connections, so make sure your messages feel personal <u>and not spammy.</u>

2. **LinkedIn Groups**: Joining and actively participating in LinkedIn groups relevant to your trip's niche can be a gold mine of potential attendees. Share useful articles, answer queries, engage in conversations, and subtly promote your trip. <u>Be a valuable member first,</u> and a promoter second.

Facebook

Facebook is our perfect platform for **community building**. Whether it's through a dedicated page or a group, Facebook gives you the chance to build a community around your trip.

1. **Facebook Groups:** Start a group for your trip and invite interested individuals. Foster a sense of community by posting engaging content, answering questions, and responding to comments. Remember to keep promotional content to a minimum and focus on providing value.

2. **Types of Posts:** Strike a balance between three types of posts:

   - **Experience Posts:** Share your experiences, stories, learnings, and insights. This builds trust and positions you as an experienced TripLeader.

   - **Value Posts:** Provide free, helpful content. Tips, recommendations, resources, guides – anything that your potential trip-goers would find useful.

- **Promotion Posts:** These are your sales pitches. Keep these to a minimum and ensure they are backed up by plenty of Experience and Value posts.

3. **Engaging with Posts and Comments:** When people comment on your posts, engage with them. This could be as simple as responding to their queries or using their comment as a launchpad to share more details about your trip, thereby sparking conversation and further interest.

4. **Some Facebook groups to join**: 'Digital Nomads Around the World,' 'Digital Nomads Spain (Malaga),' 'Remote Work & Jobs for Digital Nomads,' 'Work & Travel from anywhere,' and 'Digital Nomads Bali.' Participate in these groups, engage in discussions, publish posts, and subtly share details about your co-working trip.

Instagram

Instagram is your go-to platform for **visual storytelling**. Share eye-catching images of your destination, behind-the-scenes snapshots of trip preparations, and sneak peeks of planned activities. Instagram Stories offer an informal and interactive medium for real-time updates and candid moments

Content Creation Tips for Instagram: Platforms like **Canva** and **Adobe Spark Post** provide easy-to-use templates for creating aesthetic Instagram posts. Remember, consistency in style and tone can enhance your brand recognition. Apps like **Preview** or **Planoly** can help you plan and visualize your Instagram feed beforehand.

Here's a **step-by-step guide** to creating an Instagram post using <u>Canva</u>:

1. Start by visiting Canva's website and creating a free account if you don't already have one. You can sign up using your Google or Facebook account, or your email.

2. Once you're logged in, click on the "Create a design" button on the top-right corner of the screen. In the dropdown menu, select "Instagram Post," which will provide you with the right dimensions.

3. Now you'll see a blank canvas on the left and a variety of templates on the right. You can choose a template that suits your brand's aesthetic or create a design from scratch.

4. If you choose a template, you can customize it by clicking on the elements you want to change. You can edit text, change font style and size, alter colors, and add your images.

5. To add your images, click on the "Uploads" button on the left sidebar, and upload your photos. Drag and drop the images onto your design.

6. After you've finished designing, click on the "Download" button on the top-right corner to save your design to your computer.

7. Now, you can upload your design to Instagram. If you're using a computer, you'll need to send your image to your phone because Instagram's primary functionality is on mobile.

To learn Canva in depth, visit their "**Learn**" section. Here you'll find a series of tutorials on topics ranging from graphic design basics to specific tasks within the platform. There are also numerous YouTube tutorials for specific Canva tasks.

Meetup: Connecting with Like-minded Individuals

Much like a lively festival where different clubs gather, Meetup is a digital platform that facilitates **group meetings in person or virtually,** based on shared interests. Imagine using Meetup to assemble a troop of intrepid digital nomads, all set for a co-working adventure. Sound enticing? Hold on tight, as we're about to embark on a thrilling journey through this process!

- Kick things off by signing into Meetup. If you're a newcomer, fret not! Creating an account is a breeze, either via your trusted email or through Facebook or Google accounts.

- Once you're in, it's time for a treasure hunt! Use the search function like a sonar, seeking out groups that align with your target demographic. It could be grouped buzzing about the digital nomad lifestyle, remote work, or even travel and entrepreneurship.

- When you find a group that sets your heart racing, it's time to take the plunge! Click on the 'Join this group' button, and just like that, you're part of the team. Bear in mind, some groups might want to get acquainted with you before rolling out the welcome mat – kind of like waiting for the bouncer's approval at a high-end club!

- Now the real fun begins – event planning! Reach out to the group's organizer, present your grand vision, and extend an invitation to host an event. Be sure to underscore how their members could find your event captivating and advantageous. Remember, it's all about offering value!

- Once you get the green light from the organizer (and they often agree when they foresee a riveting event on the horizon), they will either create the event themselves or allow you to don the event-planner cap.

- As you craft the event, envision it as your personalized invitation card. Make it engaging, enticing, and most importantly, irresistible! Share all the enticing tidbits about your co-working trip. And if you have any captivating visuals or videos, don't hesitate to show them off!

- Once your event (or should we say, party) goes live, gear up for some networking! Engage with interested members, address their queries, and fuel their enthusiasm. Encourage them to RSVP and prep for an unforgettable event!

Remember, while you're part of someone else's group, respect the house rules, just as you would at a friend's soiree. No one appreciates a spammy Sam or a pushy Paula. Be authentic, provide value, and above all, have fun! You're here to forge connections and spread the cheer of your co-working trip. So, equip yourself with the tools, map out your strategy, and set forth on your adventure. **Happy TripLeading!**

CHAPTER 9

THE ESSENTIAL ROLE OF A TRIPLEADER

Okay, picture this: a funky hat, an unmissable Hawaiian shirt, and a contagious smile that could light up any room. No, we're not talking about your hip grandpa on vacation. This could be you, embracing the vibrant role of a TripLeader. But don't worry, you don't necessarily need the wild attire (unless that's your thing, then by all means, rock it). What you truly need is a captivating spirit and a heart ready to lead. Being a TripLeader isn't just about leading the way; it's about being the heart, the spark, **the Maestro of this travel symphony.**

9.1 Responsibilities and Key Qualities of a Successful TripLeader

- **The Master Planner**: As a TripLeader, you're not just a trip manager; you're the architect of memories. Your mission? <u>To</u>

choreograph unforgettable experiences. This means you're the one taking care of logistics, organizing thrill-inducing activities, and most importantly, ensuring that everyone's having the time of their lives. You've got to be nimble, good at hatching plans, sticking to them, and when the situation calls for it, letting them fly out the window!

- **People Whisperer**: Let's face it, playing puppeteer with a diverse group of soon-to-be-friends is a skill of its own. You need to don the cap of diplomat, counselor, and cheerleader, all while maintaining the balance of group dynamics. Your role is to keep morale high, resolve any conflicts (because, let's be real, they're bound to pop up), and ensure that everyone is content and comfortable. It's a bit like taming lions, but with less growling and more laughter.

- **Adaptability Guru**: The world of travel loves to surprise - think of it as its version of an impromptu comedy act. As a successful TripLeader, you'll need to adapt to these curveballs as gracefully as a ballet dancer. Whether it's a sudden change in weather or an unexpected local event, your ability to think on your feet, make swift decisions, and keep your cool will be your superpower.

9.2 The Art of Communication and Leadership in Trip Leading

Think of leading a trip as conducting a grand symphony. **Each participant, with their unique rhythm, contributes to the beautiful melody of the journey.** Orchestrating this harmony relies heavily on your ability to communicate effectively and demonstrate leadership skills.

1. **Clear Communication**: Clarity is your magic wand. Clear and concise instructions, delivered with respect and understanding, ensure smooth sailing. Your words will guide the participants, helping them understand the plan and their role in it.

2. **The Leadership Dance**: It's a tango between leading and stepping back. Knowing when to take charge and when to let the group take the reins is essential. It's about empowering your group while also guiding them.

3. **Active Listening**: Make sure everyone is heard. Encourage group discussions and private check-ins to understand the needs and concerns of the group. Listening is an underrated leadership skill, but it's the key to building trust and rapport.

4. **Cool Under Fire**: It's all about maintaining your cool when the unexpected swings by to say hello. As the TripLeader, your reaction sets the tone for the group. A calm response to

unforeseen situations reassures the group and keeps the vibe positive.

Remember, as the TripLeader, you're not just someone who knows the directions. You're the **pulse**, the **vibe**, and the **core** of the journey. Your job is to ensure that everyone not only arrives at the destination but enjoys the ride. Your success is measured not just in miles traveled, but in smiles shared, stories created, and memories made. So get ready, TripLeaders, to spread your unique charm and take your troupe on an unforgettable adventure. They're counting on you!

9.3 Managing Potential Issues and Conflicts

Now, this might come as a shock, but not everyone will be happy 100% of the time. I know, I know, it's a mind-blowing revelation. However, a key part of being a TripLeader is knowing how to manage these bumps on the road.

Strategies for Dealing with Disagreements and Conflicts Among TripMates

The first rule of handling conflicts is acknowledging that they will happen. When they do, keep these things in mind:

1. **Listen**: Everyone wants to feel heard. Let everyone involved express their feelings and perspectives. Remember, you're not just a TripLeader, but also a mediator.

2. **Be Objective**: Do your best to view the situation objectively and make decisions that are fair and beneficial to the group as a whole. You're the impartial judge here, not the tyrant.

3. **Find a Solution**: Aim for resolution, not blame. Sometimes, it's less about who's right and more about what's best for the group.

Tips on Handling Unexpected Situations and the Importance of Adaptability

Life loves surprises, and most often, they're not the pleasant kind. Here are some tips on handling these unexpected situations:

1. **Stay Calm:** Your reaction will set the tone for the group. A calm and collected response will reassure your trip mates and help manage the situation better.

2. **Adapt:** Unexpected situations demand flexibility. Whether it's a change in weather or a closed attraction, quickly come up with a Plan B (or C or D, if necessary).

Remember, as a TripLeader, you're the captain of the ship. Your ability to manage conflicts and handle unexpected situations will greatly enhance the overall trip experience for your group and make you a legendary TripLeader.

CHAPTER 10

CASTING THE PERFECT ENSEMBLE FOR YOUR TRIP

Just like casting for a Broadway show, selecting the right TripMates is about balance. Not everyone can play the lead, and not every understudy stays in the background. So, without further ado, welcome to your casting director boot camp!

10.1 The Red Flags: Auditioning Your Potential TripMates

Treat every interaction like an audition. You're on the lookout for the superstars, the supporting actors, and those who might not be ready for the limelight just yet. Here's what to watch for:

1. **Negative Attitude:** Complainers can turn a sunny beach into a gloomy basement quicker than a tropical storm. If they grumble more than they giggle, take note.

2. **Self-centeredness**: Ensemble cast, remember? If they continuously pivot the conversation back to themselves, it might hint at a one-man-show mentality.

3. **Unpredictability**: You're assembling a team that can rely on each other. If they're frequently late, often rescheduling, or struggling to commit to plans, it could hint at potential reliability issues on the trip.

10.2 The Art of the Video Call: Directing Your Way to Success**

Yes, it's an art, and we're about to turn you into Picasso with a headset.

1. **Preparation**: Arm yourself with knowledge. Familiarize yourself with their profile before the call.

2. **Set the Stage**: Start with a smile - remember, first impressions last! Be warm and welcoming as you start the call.

3. **Break the Ice**: Engage in some small talk. Ask about their location, the weather, how their day's been or anything specific in their room.

4. **The Personal Monologue**: Get them talking about their past travels, their job, their interests. This will also give you a glimpse into their lifestyle.

5. **Share Your Own Act:** Give them a brief about your journey, your experiences.

6. **The Trip Pitch**: Lay down your cards. Share about the trip, the planned activities, the locations, the villa details, right down to the daily routine.

7. **The Ensemble**: Share about the potential group members. Talk about their countries, ages, gender, and jobs. Paint a picture of a diverse and exciting group.

8. **Callbacks**: If all goes well, guide them about the next steps. Where can they find more information? When do they need to confirm?

9. **Share the Script**: Post-call, share all relevant links and information for them to go through.

10. **A Standing Ovation**: Finally, thank them for their time. A little appreciation goes a long way in creating rapport and leaving a positive impression, even if they don't end up joining the trip.

11. **Curtain Call**: Ensure them that you're available if they have any more questions, and don't hesitate to follow up.

10.3 The Director's Cut: Politely Declining
a Potential TripMate

If you feel they're not the right fit, be honest but diplomatic. Phrases like, "I think the trip might not align with your expectations," or "I'm afraid the group dynamics might not be what you're looking for," can work. Remember, it's better to be upfront now than face issues during the trip.

And, always end on a positive note. They may not be a fit for this trip, but who knows about the next one? Maintaining these relationships could lead to a surprise casting success in the future.

By using these strategies, you won't just assemble a team for your trip - you'll curate a cast for the adventure of a lifetime!

CHAPTER 11

THE CASH ADVENTURE - EARNINGS AS A TRIPLEADER

L adies and gentlemen, pack your financial compass and hiking boots. We're about to embark on the thrilling, occasionally uphill but always rewarding journey of understanding the economic side of the Co-Working Trip. As the savvy TripLeader you're becoming, you must be ready to navigate the landscape of costs, learn the art of pricing, and unlock the treasure chest of income sources. And what better way to illustrate this than by taking a (virtual) detour to the sunny shores of Cyprus?

11.1 Mapping the Route: Expected Costs**

Every great adventure starts with a solid plan, and for our money-making journey, that plan is a well-crafted budget. Let's break down the components:

The Shelter (Accommodation): The grand palace or a cozy villa, your choice of accommodation, may cost you anywhere from 2000€ to 5000€. But hold onto your wallets! No need to empty your coffers right at the start. You might be able to book the accommodation and kick off the trip selling process without paying a dime upfront, reducing your initial investment to a mere 10-15% of the total cost. That's what I call smart spending!

The Voyage and Survival (Flight tickets and Personal Expenses): Don't forget to factor in your round-trip tickets and living expenses. After all, a TripLeader can't lead on an empty stomach, right?

So, with a bit of savvy and strategy, you can get your co-working trip rolling with minimal investment and maximum excitement.

11.2 The Art of Bartering: Pricing Strategies**

Setting the perfect price for your co-working trip is like finding the sweet spot between a sizzling deal and a decent paycheck. Here's the alchemy behind the process:

- *Accommodation*: That's your base price - the cost for either a shared or private room for 2 weeks.

- *Transportation*: Are you planning to rent a horse-drawn carriage (or, more likely, a car)? Decide whether to include this in the final price or to split it later with your TripMates.

- *Your Expenses*: Factor in your costs for the voyage and survival, add up all your expected expenses, and divide it by the number of TripMates you are targeting.

- *Buffer*: You never know when you might encounter a surprise - a 10% buffer should take care of any pesky dragons (or unexpected expenses).

- *Your Fee*: The crowning glory of your calculations. How much gold do you want to add to your coffers? This amount is entirely up to you - but remember to keep it reasonable.

Remember, your co-working trip price is like a magic potion - it should attract many willing travelers without emptying their pockets. Charging a bit less on your first few quests is not a bad strategy for luring more adventurers.

11.3 Unlocking the Treasure Chest: Income Sources**

Your reward as a TripLeader comes from the fee that you sprinkle on top of the base price. This fee is your treasure - the golden fruit of your hard work and creativity. The more unique and magical the journey you offer, the bigger the treasure you can claim.

Let's bring this to life with a little tale from the sun-drenched Mediterranean.

**Showcase: A Tale of Cyprus **

Imagine we're on a quest in Cyprus, in a seafront villa with five cozy bedrooms. Our costs totaled 3000€, including 2500€ for the villa, 200€ for flights, and 300€ for living expenses.

We recruited a band of ten eager adventurers, each contributing 770€ to our quest. So, the coffers filled up with 7700€. After paying off our expenses of 3000

€, we're left with a treasure of 4700€.

Now, don't we all love a story with a happy ending and pockets full of gold?

While our tale is just a mock-up (based on real-life possibilities), it does illustrate the earning potential as a TripLeader. Every co-working trip is its own unique adventure, with its own unique financial structure.

Being a TripLeader isn't just about crafting unforgettable experiences. It's also about learning to navigate the financial waters, strategizing your path, and coming out with a treasure at the end. The money-making journey awaits you, fellow adventurer! Are you ready to set sail?

CHAPTER 12

DIGITAL NOMAD MASTERY: ESSENTIAL TOOLS AND PENNY-WISE PRACTICES

Greetings, digital explorers! Prepare to dive into a world of virtual efficiency and savvy budgeting. We're about to unleash some priceless advice, served with a side of humor. So buckle up!

12.1. Essential Kit for the Tech-Savvy Nomad

Think of your digital tools as your superhero sidekicks. They're here to streamline your life, keeping you organized and worry-free:

1. **NomadList & RemoteYear**: Your go-to platforms for scouting future co-working spots. NomadList grades cities based on vital factors such as cost of living, internet speed, and climate, among others. In contrast, RemoteYear simplifies

your planning process by providing pre-set itineraries for an entire year.

2. **Teleport & NomadRest**: Can't decide where to live and work next? Teleport provides a comprehensive analysis of hundreds of cities worldwide, from the cost of living to the quality of life and safety standards. NomadRest is the digital nomad's home away from home, offering accommodation options specifically designed for remote workers like you.

3. **Tripit**: Managing multiple travel plans can be as tricky as juggling flaming torches. Thankfully, Tripit acts as your personal assistant, organizing all your travel plans in one easy-to-access place.

But that's not all. We've also got you covered when it comes to insurance:

1. **World Nomads & Safetywing:** These two services understand the unique needs of digital nomads, providing comprehensive coverage for everything from health emergencies to equipment loss.

2. **Travelex:** Life is unpredictable, especially when traveling. Travelex offers trip insurance to cover cancellations, interruptions, and more.

When it comes to productivity, we've got some game-changers for you:

1. **Notion & TickTick**: Notion is your all-in-one workspace, perfect for writing, planning, and organizing, while TickTick acts as your personal task manager, ensuring you never miss a deadline.

2. **PomoDone App & Stayfocusd**: Maximize productivity with the PomoDone app, integrating with your existing tasks and using the Pomodoro technique to keep you focused. Stay focused is your ally in battling distractions, limiting your time on non-work related websites.

12.2 Budgeting & Savings: The Path to Financial Freedom

Strap on your money-saving boots, folks. We're about to embark on an adventure through the land of savvy spending:

A. The Secret Art of Flight Booking:

1. **Incognito Mode**: Use your browser's incognito mode when searching for flights. It's like being a secret agent, preventing those pesky websites from tracking your searches and hiking prices.

2. **Skyscanner & eDreams**: These are your private flight investigators, helping you find the best and cheapest options. Skyscanner even suggests different stopovers for extra savings!

3. **Ryanair Trick:** Wait until the end of the checkout process to select the 'Priority & 2 Cabin Bags' option. It's like finding a hidden discount!

4. **Price Alert:** Enable this feature on flight booking platforms to get notifications when prices drop. It's like having a personal stockbroker for flight prices!

B. Airbnb: A Treasure Trove of Savings:

1. **Picture Hunting & Profile Investigation:** Put on your detective hat and investigate all the property pictures and the owner's profile. You might find some clues about direct contact or even a discounted deal.

2. **Bold Messaging:** If you're feeling adventurous, negotiate directly with the property owner for better prices. Or, in a bold move, try to sneak your contact information into the conversation!

C. Loyalty Programs and Deals: Your Secret Weapon:

1. **Frequent Flyer & Hotel Loyalty Programs:** American Airlines' "AAdvantage" and Delta's "SkyMiles" are your tickets to earning rewards on flights, while the Marriott Bonvoy program could score you free WiFi and mobile check-in, amongst other benefits.

2. **Credit Card Points & Deal-Scouting Websites:** The Chase Sapphire Preferred Card is a gold mine for travel

rewards. For deal scouting, Hopper and Skyscanner are your best friends, predicting future prices and notifying you when it's time to buy.

3. **Newsletter Subscriptions & Loyalty Program Aggregators:** Scott's Cheap Flights sends hot flight deals to your inbox, and AwardWallet keeps all your loyalty programs organized in one place.

4. **Cash Back Programs:** Rakuten provides cash back, deals, and discounts on over 2,500 stores.

With these tools in your arsenal and these money-saving hacks at your fingertips, you're all set for your nomadic journey. The road ahead is full of efficiency, savings, and unlimited adventure. Happy traveling!

CHAPTER 13

FINAL PREPARATIONS, ENJOYING THE JOURNEY, AND LOOKING AHEAD

You've made it! From dreaming about that perfect trip to finding your travel mates, from marketing the experience to booking the perfect villa, every step has been a part of this journey. But remember, the journey is far from over. It's time for final preparations, living the adventure, and then paving the path for future escapades.

13.1 Setting the Stage: The WhatsApp Group

A successful trip thrives on clear communication and bonding. Start by creating a WhatsApp group. This is the digital campfire around which everyone gathers, sharing updates, clarifying doubts, and forging connections even before the trip begins. Here's how to make the most of this platform:

1. Create the group and add all your TripMates.

2. Break the ice by introducing yourself. Share your excitement about the trip, express your gratitude for their trust in you, and invite them to share their anticipation.

3. Encourage everyone to introduce themselves with a few prompts like:

   - Who are you?

   - Where are you from?

   - What's your job?

   - Anything interesting/funny/legit you want to share about you?

   - Your flight arrival time and location

   - Your flight back (if you already have it)

You can also take this as an opportunity to set some ground rules, such as respecting others' privacy and avoiding offensive language. This fosters a sense of community and establishes the norms for a harmonious trip.

13.2 The Journey Begins: Helping with Transfers

Imagine landing in a foreign place, maybe even for the first time, with excitement mixed with nervousness. As a TripLeader, you can make this transition smoother for your TripMates. Research the best ways to get from the airport to your accommodation. Look for options like local transportation, shared cabs, or maybe even hiring a minivan if the group's arrival times are close. Your TripMates will appreciate the effort, and it'll get the trip off to a great start.

13.3 The Art of Enjoying the Journey

Now comes the most rewarding part—living the journey. As you visit places, savor cuisines, and share laughter, remember to stay present. These moments and these connections are what make this whole endeavor worthwhile.

Encourage your TripMates to share their experiences and pictures in the WhatsApp group. This not only strengthens the bond within the group but also creates a treasure trove of memories and promotional content for your future trips.

Packing for Success

No one wants to be the person who forgets their charger or sunscreen. So, share a comprehensive packing list in your WhatsApp group. Remember to tailor it according to your destination and planned activities. It might seem trivial, but your TripMates will thank you when they don't have to scramble for a hat in the scorching sun.

13.4 The Journey Continues: The Coaching Program

The end of your trip is just the beginning of countless other adventures. For those who've caught the travel bug and wish to continue leading trips, we offer a comprehensive coaching program.

This program provides in-depth training, mentorship, and resources to turn you from a one-time TripLeader to a seasoned pro. It's designed to equip you with skills and insights that extend beyond what we've covered in this book, diving deeper into the nuances of trip-leading.

Remember, this journey you've embarked on isn't just about seeing the world. It's about embracing a lifestyle that champions flexibility, adventure, and connection. And as you progress on this path, remember to enjoy every step, every misstep, and everything in between. Because that's what makes this journey truly unforgettable.

Keep the spirit of exploration alive, and here's to many more adventures. Saludos!

EMBRACE THE ADVENTURE

And there we have it, folks! This is the end of our journey through this book, but remember, it's the start of an even bigger adventure for you. As you close this last chapter, you stand on the threshold of becoming not just a digital nomad but a beacon for others yearning for similar experiences.

Throughout our exploration, we've delved into everything from crafting your dream journey to perfecting video call interviews; from conquering marketing fears to wrestling with budgeting apps; from basking in the joy of the actual travel experience to the exhilarating potential of leading your own trips. Each chapter, each concept, has been a stepping stone towards a life of **freedom, exploration,** and **connection**.

I still remember the first time I stepped off the plane in Sicily. The air was salty and warm, the bustling streets were alive with energy, and my heart was thudding with a mixture of excitement and fear. But as I navigated through foreign lands, met incredible people, and dealt with unexpected curveballs, I came to realize that it wasn't just about the trip; it was about the journey within myself. That's the secret sauce, my friends!

Now, I have a confession to make. This book isn't your typical travel guide. Heck, it isn't even your average digital nomad manual. It's a **call-to-adventure**, a passport to a new lifestyle, a blueprint for a community that defies geographical boundaries. If there's anything I want you to remember from this book, it's this - *travel is a mindset, not just an activity.* Embrace the chaos, celebrate the unexpected, and remember, we're all just adventurers figuring things out one trip at a time.

So here's my parting wisdom, gleaned from numerous trips, countless flight tickets, and some serious sunburns - travel like you mean it. Don't just dip your toes in; dive headfirst into the experience. Savor the local cuisine (even if you can't pronounce it), participate in those weird and wonderful traditions (dancing around in circles can be surprisingly liberating), engage in deep conversations with locals (yes, those hand gestures do make sense), and most importantly, embrace the changes within you.

You might start as a novice traveler, but before you know it, you'll be the one leading others into the thrilling world of digital nomadism. And as you embark on this journey, remember - in the grand scheme of things, we're all just fellow travelers spinning around on this beautiful blue marble in the vast expanse of the universe. So, why not make this journey count?

Remember, as you step into this adventure, you're not alone. We are a community, a tribe of global explorers, weaving stories and shared experiences across the vast canvas of the world. Our medium? Travel. Our canvas? Every corner of the globe. Why not create a narrative that's vivid, packed with adventure, and that's uniquely your own?

So, fellow explorer, pack your suitcase, make sure your passport's in hand, and gear up for a life that's not just extraordinary, but also filled with excitement and enlightenment. The world eagerly anticipates your footprints, and your heart yearns for the exhilaration of fresh experiences.

In this journey, you're not just an observer, but an active participant. The power to shape your narrative lies in your hands. And just like any good narrative, it can be filled with twists, turns, and learning experiences. That's where our coaching program comes in. Think of it as a compass, guiding you as you navigate the exciting world of co-working travel. Our program doesn't just prepare you for the journey, but also ensures you make the most of it.

So, are you ready to take that plunge? Your digital nomad adventure awaits, filled with unwritten stories, undiscovered locales, and unmade connections. I can't wait to hear your tales, learn from your encounters, and cheer for your voyage.

Here's to your extraordinary journey! , And as we say in Italian, **'Saluti e buon Viaggio** – cheers and safe travels!

Un abbraccio,

www.ingramcontent.com/pod-product-compliance
Lightning Source LLC
Chambersburg PA
CBHW062357290526
45794CB00005B/2272

* 9 7 9 8 8 5 8 0 0 6 5 9 6 *